# CONTENTS

# PREFACE

Houghton Mifflin Company publishes outstanding education textbooks in the areas of foundations of education, introduction to education, educational psychology, special education, and early childhood education. These textbooks introduce students to many concepts, policies, and research that undergird educational practice. However, as is the case for virtually all introductory texts, many topics are introduced but not covered in great depth. The Houghton Mifflin Teacher Education Guide Series is designed to provide more in-depth coverage of selected educational topics studied in the teacher education curriculum.

At the present time there are five guides in the series:

- Diversity in the Classroom

- Classroom Assessment

- Inclusion

- Technology Tools

- School-based Interventions

The topics for these guides were selected because they are addressed in virtually all teacher education programs, and contain vital information for beginning teachers if they are to be successful in the classroom. Instructors may use the guides either for required or enrichment reading.

Each of these guides provides pre-service teachers with greater in-depth knowledge, application suggestions, and additional resources on its particular topic. All the guides share a common format that includes an introduction to the topic, knowledge that the prospective teacher should possess about the topic, examples of and suggestions for how the knowledge can be applied, and both print and Web-based resources for further exploration. Each guide also contains 10–15 questions designed to help the prospective teacher reflect on the concepts and ideas introduced in the guide, as well as a glossary of key terms.

 HOUGHTON MIFFLIN GUIDE

SERIES

# An Educator's Guide to
# **Technology Tools**

Cheryl Mason Bolick
The University of North Carolina at Chapel Hill

James M. Cooper, Series Editor
University of Virginia

HOUGHTON MIFFLIN COMPANY     BOSTON   NEW YORK

Senior Sponsoring Editor: Sue Pulvermacher-Alt
Senior Development Editor: Lisa Mafrici
Editorial Associate: Sara Hauschildt
Editorial Assistant: Liliana Ritter
Manufacturing Manager: Florence Cadran
Marketing Manager: Nicola Poser

Printed in the U.S.A.

ISBN: 0-618-31324-9

123456789-CRS-06 05 04 03 02

The use of computer technology in schools has increased dramatically in recent years and shows few signs of slowing down. Obtaining hardware and software is always a challenge for schools, but an even bigger challenge is helping teachers to use technology in ways that improve student learning. In this guide, Cheryl Mason Bolick explores different methods and tools teachers can use to develop an effective classroom learning environment for students of the digital generation. Moving from a teacher-centered environment to one in which students use technology to gather, analyze, and evaluate information, students learn to create new knowledge and to become critical thinkers by having greater control over their learning. Teachers can also use technology to increase their own productivity. Knowing how to use these technology tools effectively is a critical skill for teachers in the 21st century.

# PART I: INTRODUCTION

## TEACHING AND LEARNING WITH TODAY'S TECHNOLOGY TOOLS

The first morning bell rings and the students begin to file into Ms. Lane's seventh grade classroom. As the students settle in for the day they hang their coats in the classroom closet and pull their handheld computing devices out of their backpacks. Each cluster of desks has a computer with a device attached for synching information to and from the handheld. The students synch their **handhelds** and send their homework assignments and any notes from home to their teacher, while at the same time they download the handouts for the day's activities.

As the second bell rings, Ms. Lane asks the students to open the current events assignment on their handhelds. Ms. Lane has given the students web-based news sources from around the globe to read and summarize. Using their wireless handhelds, the students read their news clips and then join a class discussion about the day's current events and the media's interpretation of these events.

---

### A Closer Look     Handheld Computing Devices

Most handhelds today are as long as an index card and as thick as a student's assignment pad. Prices range from $100 to $700. Software has been developed that permit handheld users to perform virtually every task that they could perform on their laptop or desktop computer.

Using their handhelds, students can create word-processed documents, enter data into spreadsheets, search databases, search the **Web** and send **e-mails**. Peripherals for handhelds extend the potential applications of the handheld. Peripherals include collapsible keyboards, global positioning systems, digital cameras, phones, audio recorders, and MP3 players.

---

After completing the current events activity, Ms. Lane asks the students to pull up their rainfall data from science class. The students quickly go to the interactive web site where they have been inputting environmental data and comparing it with student data from classrooms around the world.

Ms. Lane explains to the students that today they are going to continue their collaborative writing activity. In this activity, students synthesize the environmental data and collaboratively write five paragraph essays. In groups of three, students use the keyboard to collectively write the introductory paragraph on their handheld. The students spend the rest of the class period highly engaged in analyzing the different data sets and describing their findings in their essay.

Moments before the bell rings, Ms. Lane reminds the students to check their assignment sheets on their handhelds. There, she has prepared instructions for the students explaining that they will each write one paragraph of the essay for homework. Tomorrow in class they will beam their individual paragraphs to their group members and collaboratively write the concluding paragraph. The bell rings and the students quickly pack up their belongings and head to their next class.

Handheld devices and the **Internet** are just two technology tools that are transforming teaching and learning. From a small network of 23 computers in 1973 to the millions of networked computers today, technology is empowering teachers and students to revolutionize instruction. With the nearly ubiquitous access to the Internet in today's classrooms, the promise of technology to enhance learning is greater than ever; however, even though the majority of students use the Internet for school, this use occurs primarily outside of their classrooms and is outside the direction of their teachers (Levin & Arafeh, 2002). To best prepare students to be successful in our information-rich global society, teachers must understand the power and potential of technology tools.

## Digital Classrooms

The printing press, camera, film projector, television, and VCR each have transformed education in unique ways. Likewise, revolutionary developments in today's field of technology are bringing drastic changes to the way we communicate with one another, the way we work, and the way we learn. Today's generation of students live in a society that surrounds them with audio, video, and interactive media. According to the Kaiser Family Foundation's study on children's use of computers (1999), nearly seven in ten kids have a computer at home and nearly half have Internet access from home. Many of today's students come to school expecting to use computers in their classrooms.

Classroom teachers must be prepared to provide their students with access to technology that enriches learning opportunities. Students need to develop skills that will allow them to be successful in today's technology-driven global economy. The most basic of these skills include manipulating data in a spreadsheet, developing multimedia presentations, or typing a word-processed document.

More than helping students develop basic computer literacy, however, today's teachers also should be prepared to help students gather, analyze, and evaluate information. Students must be able to use the information they find to become effective problem-solvers and critical thinkers. This Guide will explore different methods and tools teachers may use to develop an effective classroom learning environment for students of the digital generation.

The portrayal of Ms. Lane's classroom is a realistic scenario of technology tools being used to enhance classroom learning. Today, there are classrooms of varying grade levels using handhelds in similar lessons. It is essential to note that student learning is enhanced not just by the technology tools, but also by Ms. Lane's effective pedagogy. She planned her classroom carefully to be a student-centered classroom that promotes critical and higher-order thinking.

Technology tools such as the handheld computer are changing the face of today's classroom by offering teachers and students tools that can help teachers make the transition from traditional, teacher-centered environments to new learning environments. In order for students to learn with technology, however, teachers must understand how to create learning environments that promote meaningful and authentic learning. The International Society for Technology in Education (ISTE) has developed a series of standards to guide teachers as they learn not only how to use technology, but also how technology can be used to create new learning environments.

## National Educational Technology Standards

Most states have technology competency requirements for both pre-service and in-service teachers. These standards follow closely the

ISTE's National Educational Technology Standards (NETS). ISTE has developed standards for both K–12 students and standards for teachers.

NETS are organized into six categories of performance indicators for classroom teachers: technology operations and concepts; planning and designing learning environments and experiences; teaching, learning and the curriculum; assessment and evaluation; productivity and professional practice; and social, ethical, legal and human issues. The NETS writing team has prepared a series of K–12 content-based lessons for each indicator. These lesson plans are available on the NETS web page (http://www.iste.org) or in the NETS printed publication.

---

**A Closer Look    Sample NETS Lessons**

- *Trigonometric Tables: Tangent:* Students enter data from rocket launches in Geometer's Sketchpad software to develop an understanding of the tangent table.
- *Who's in Control Here?* Simulation software and Internet resources provide students with information in which they must make decisions about sovereignty.
- *Electronic Book Discussion:* Students engage in an online threaded discussion after reading assigned books to further their understanding of the text and to promote equity among all students.
- *Cool Liquids:* Students record temperatures on their graphing calculators or a spreadsheet to develop an understanding of evaporation.

# PART II: KNOWLEDGE

## STUDENT LEARNING TOOLS

Schools are more high-tech today than they have ever been. Nationally, there are just over four students for every instructional school computer and the number of students per Internet-connected computer in schools dropped from 7.9 in 2000 to 6.8 in 2001 (Skinner, 2002). Beyond having access to computers, schools report that a majority of their teachers used the Internet for instruction. Given the increase in access to computers and reports of teacher usage, can one assume that technology is enhancing teaching and learning?

Unfortunately, we cannot. Many teachers are not using technology effectively. That is, many teachers use technology for technology's sake, rather than using technology to create meaningful learning environments. For example, drill and practice or playing math games are the most frequently reported uses of computers for math instruction (Skinner, 2002) rather than using technology tools to create student-centered learning environments.

### ESTABLISHING NEW LEARNING ENVIRONMENTS
#### Incorporating New Strategies (NETS, 2002)

| Traditional Learning ⟶ Environments | New Learning Environments |
|---|---|
| Teacher-centered instruction | Student-centered learning |
| Single sense stimulation | Multisensory stimulation |
| Single path progression | Multipath progression |
| Single media | Multimedia |
| Isolated work | Collaborative work |
| Information delivery | Information exchange |
| Passive learning | Active/exploratory/inquiry-based learning |
| Factual, knowledge-based learning | Critical thinking and informed decision-making |
| Reactive response | Proactive/planned action |
| Isolated, artificial context | Authentic, real-world context |

Teachers make decisions every day about how best to help their students learn. Before using technology tools in the classroom, teachers should ask themselves the following two questions (Harris, 1998):

1.  Will technology allow me to do something with my students that I could not before technology?

2.  Will technology allow me to do something with my students better than I'm doing it now?

## Extending Classroom Learning Through the Internet

The Internet has opened classroom doors to resources that were not available to most classrooms. From paintings, books, and maps to movie clips, teachers and students can access thousands of resources that can be used to enhance classroom learning. These resources can either be online documents and data housed on the Internet or people who communicate through the Internet.

### Online Research

In 1993, there were approximately 130 web sites; today there are hundreds of millions (Leiner, et al., 2000). These web sites provide teachers and students greater access to sources that otherwise would not be available for classroom learning. The table below highlights online resources available for various content areas that were not accessible by most teachers and students before the Internet.

| A Closer Look | Online Content Area Resources |
|---|---|
| Content Area | Sample Online Resources |
| English / Language Arts | Mark Twain in His Times<br>        http://etext.lib.virginia.edu/railton/<br>Aesop's Fables<br>        http://www.aesopfables.com/ |
| Science | Science Junction<br>        http://www.ncsu.edu/sciencejunction/<br>Science Learning Network<br>        http://www.sln.org/ |

| A Closer Look | Online Content Area Resources |
|---|---|
| **Content Area** | **Sample Online Resources** |
| **Mathematics** | The Math Forum <br>         http://mathforum.org/ <br> MicroWorlds Math Library <br>         http://www.microworlds.com/library/math/ |
| **Health / Physical Education** | PE Central <br>         http://www.pecentral.org/ <br> Kids Health <br>         http://www.kidshealth.org/ |
| **Social Studies** | American Memory Project <br>         http://memory.loc.gov/ <br> History Matters <br>         http://historymatters.gmu.edu/ |
| **Art** | Smithsonian American Art Museum <br>         http://www.nmaa.si.edu/ <br> Art Safari <br>         http://www.moma.org/onlineprojects/artsafari/ <br>         index.html |
| **Music / Performing Arts** | Instrument Encyclopedia <br>         http://www.si.umich.edu/chico/instrument/ <br> The Drama Collection <br>         http://eserver.org/drama/ |

The number of online resources available to enrich classroom learning today is phenomenal. Yet, the vast number of resources on the Internet can often seem unwieldy. Given that there are well over 500 billion documents on the Internet (Bergman, 2000), teachers must be prepared to teach their students effective research skills. Online research skills are important skills that students will use for a lifetime.

There are two types of search engines for identifying resources on the web: mechanical search engines and human-operated directories. Mechanical search engines use web robots to automatically search the web. Alta Vista (http://www.altavista.com) and Google (http://www.google.com) are examples of mechanical search engines. Human cataloguers, on the other hand, generate human-operated directories by using virtual libraries and categories of resources. Yahoo (http://www.yahoo.com) is an example of a human-operated directory.

When deciding which search engine to use, factors such as the size of the database, speed of the search process and frequency of updating should be considered. Frequency is an important factor because a search of the web is not a search of everything that is on the web at that given time, but rather, a search of the documents that were on the web the last time the database was uploaded.

There are a number of helpful guides and tutorials available online for teachers and students. Examples of these online guides are:

- KidsClick World of Searching
  http://www.worldsofsearching.org/

- UCBerkeley Search Strategies
  http://www.lib.berkeley.edu/TeachingLib/Guides/Internet/
  Strategies.html

| *Practical Tips and Strategies* | *Search Strategies* |
|---|---|

1. **Boolean search** operators (e.g., AND, NOT, OR, NEAR) narrow the search by limiting the number of documents that will be searched. For example, if searching for pages about William Shakespeare, you could search for either "WILLIAM AND SHAKESPEARE" or "WILLIAM NEAR SHAKESPEARE"

2. Most search engines have advanced sections that will allow you to search by "file format". This means you can search specifically for images, .pdf files, Word files, audio and video clips as well as PowerPoint presentations posted on the web.

3. Truncation and wildcards (e.g.,*) will help search for different variations of a word. For example, if looking for math lesson plans, enter "MATH*" so that the result would include all of the lesson plans with both math and mathematics in the descriptors.

# Telecollaboration

In many ways, the best resource on the Internet is other people.
**Telecollaboration** activities offer a variety of educational experiences
for students in levels K12.  Prior to the Internet, outside resources were
limited to the traditional guest speaker, field trip, or pen pal. Now,
there are voluminous ways to connect students with other people across
the globe. Using e-mail, web-based discussions and video
conferencing, teachers and students can connect in meaningful ways.

Harris' Virtual Architecture (1998) book and website are essential tools
for teachers interested in implementing telecollaborative activities. Her
work identifies three genres of telecollaborative activities:

- *Interpersonal Exchanges*: Students and teachers connect via the
  Internet with geographically disparate individuals.

- *Information Collection and Analysis:* Students gather authentic data
  and create projects to share and analyze with others.

- *Problem Solving:* Collaborative activities that engage students in
  critical thinking and problem-based learning.

Harris (1998) highlights how telecollaboration activities can benefit
global education.  It can expose students to "differing opinions,
perspectives, beliefs, experiences, and thinking processes; allow
students to compare, contrast, and/or combine similar information
collected in dissimilar locations; and provide a platform where students
can communicate with a real audience using text and imagery" (p. 55).

| *A Closer Look* | *Telecollaboration Activities* |
|---|---|
| **Activity Structures** | **Curriculum Examples** |
| **Keypals:** students correspond with a partner via e-mail over a period of time | ePals.com  is one of the largest Keypals services on the Interrnet. Teachers and students can register and connect with others across the globe to discuss a broad range of issues including: current events, Harry Potter, rainfall, or teacher professional development. http://www.epals.com/ |
| **Impersonations:** Students engage in dialogue with historical figures | Ask Thomas Jefferson is an interactive web page that allows student to pose inquiries to "Thomas Jefferson". Students and teachers can also read through the collection of letters other students have sent to the |

| A Closer Look | Telecollaboration Activities |
|---|---|
| **Activity Structures** | **Curriculum Examples** |
| | site. http://www.monticello.org/education/asktj/instructions.html |
| **Electronic Appearances:** Students communicate with experts in a particular field. | Women of NASA Chat is a web page that facilitates discussion between the Women of NASA and teachers and students. Students can e-mail individual questions or engage in scheduled real-time chats or forums. Archives of all discussions are stored on the web page, along with helpful teaching resources. http://image.gsfc.nasa.gov/poetry/ask/askmag.html |
| **Information Exchanges:** Students collect local data and share it with others. | The GLOBE Program invites teachers and students to post and collect environmental data from their communities in the data archive. Students collaborate with other students and scientists from around the globe to learn more about local and global environments. http://www.globe.gov/ |
| **Electronic Publishing:** Students create **hypertext** documents and share them with others. | MidLink is an online journal both for and by middle school students. Monthly themes are posted and students from around the world contribute poems, essays, art, and multimedia projects to be published. http://www.ncsu.edu/midlink/ |

## Legal and Ethical Issues

Although the Internet is opening classrooms to the world in many positive and meaningful ways, the Internet also presents new challenges for teachers. Educators must be aware of legal and ethical issues surrounding technology. Two of the major concerns to address are Internet safety and copyright.

Teachers must be aware of risks and areas of concern associated with children's use of the Internet. The most prevalent risks include children communicating with **cyberpredators** on the Internet and children's access of inappropriate materials on the Internet. Unfortunately, there are cases each year that involve cyberpredators interacting with students on the Internet, which may lead to children being coerced into face-to-face meetings or to the children giving personal information such as passwords or credit card numbers to strangers. Teachers should work with colleagues and parents to establish an acceptable use policy (AUP) for Internet in their classrooms. AUPs will often include guidelines regarding publishing children's photographs on the web and student access of certain web sites. Students must be taught that the Internet is a public space and that there are guidelines to ensure safe use of the space.

| Practical Tips and Strategies | Internet Safety Tips |
| --- | --- |

1. The best way to ensure that young people are having positive online experiences is to supervise their activities. Monitor students' computer activities by placing the computer in an easily viewable area. Maintain open communication about information they have found, sites they have explored, and people with whom they have chatted.
2. Investigate the use of filtering software. Even with these controls, however, teachers still need to be involved. An excellent resource regarding filters can be found at http://www.cyberangels.org/parentsguide/filtering.html
3. Establish an acceptable use policy for the Internet. The National Center for Missing and Exploited Children (http://www.missingkids.com) has created a popular brochure that outlines suggested children's rules for online safety. (Berson, et al. 2001)

Copyright is another issue that must be addressed with students. Cutting and pasting are two **web browser** and word processing features that help make the software so user-friendly. Yet, these features also make it easy for students to cite their resources. Just as it is important to cite books and periodicals when doing research, it is important to cite online resources.

Teachers should ensure that students understand the importance of giving proper credit for resources they reference or quote. Once they understand this concept, they should be presented with proper guidelines for citing work. MidLink has a helpful web page that provides guides for citing electronic resources at

http://www.ncsu.edu/midlink/citing.html. Forms to request permission
to post graphics on your web page are also found on this web page.

Teachers should also help students develop strategies that will support
their efforts of respecting copyright. One strategy is to use multiple
windows when taking notes from a web page. That is, resize the web
browser so that it vertically fits on the left half of the computer screen.
Open a word processing document and resize it so that it fits vertically
on the right half of the screen. When students use this strategy, they are
more apt to paraphrase the information they are researching, rather than
copy and paste verbatim.

# Enhancing Classroom Learning with Software

In addition to the tremendous resources available on the Internet,
educational software tools may also enhance classroom learning.
Software programs are considered either instructional software (e.g.,
simulations and tutorials) or developmental software (e.g., spreadsheets
or multimedia editing). The software industry is large and continues to
grow. Two excellent resources that have extensive software evaluation
databases are the California Learning Resource Network
(http://www.clrn.org/home/) and the Children's Software Review
(http://www2.childrenssoftware.com).

## Simulations and Tutorials

Simulations are a genre of software that engages students in real-world
problem-solving lessons that require critical thinking skills. Often, the
software employs a degree of interactivity that requires the students to
enter information throughout the simulation and respond to the
consequences of their decisions. Multimedia features, such as sound
and video, are engaging complements to the traditional text.
Simulations have been developed for each content area and grade level.

"Prime Time Math: Fire" by Tom Snyder Productions is an example of
a simulation. In this software, students assume the role of firefighters
who must make mathematical decisions to combat a burning building,
such as selecting the correct length and size of a hose and appropriate
pressure. Audio and video clips, along with narratives lead the students
through the scenario and call upon the students to apply mathematical
concepts to the situation.

"Decisions, Decisions: The Environment" by Tom Snyder Productions is another example of simulation software. Students are assigned to play the role of different individuals (scientist, a campaign manager, an environmentalist, and an economist) who are impacted by the recent pollution of a town pond. Students are presented with a series of data and documentation from which they must make public policy decisions about how to address the pollution problem.

Tutorials are a second category of educational software designed to extend classroom learning. This type of software introduces students to new information, and then provides them with opportunities to apply the new information in a self-paced fashion. Musicianship Basics by New Horizons is an example of tutorial software in which students are introduced to fundamental music reading and listening skills. As students move through the program, they respond to a series of questions. A log tracks the student responses and suggests remediation activities based on the individual student.

World History: An Interactive Approach, by WorldView Software is another example of tutorial software. Students are presented with chronologically arranged world history modules. After reading through each module, students are presented with a series of objective questions to assess whether or not they have mastered this history content.

## Development Software

Development software is specifically designed to allow teachers and students to enter and manipulate data for either individual learning or class presentation. Both categories can be used across content areas and grade levels, although there are some content-specific pieces of development software.

Spreadsheets, databases, and word processing software are generic software. That is, they are empty "shells" equipped to input numerical or textual data. Spreadsheets are designed specifically for the manipulation of numerical data. The basic function of most spreadsheets is the calculation of numerical formulas. Once data has been entered and calculated, students can choose to visually represent the data in charts or graphs. By giving students the opportunity to manipulate the data into different formats, they are able to explore the connection between numerical, algebraic and graphical representations of data.

Word processing software may be the most basic of the generic software, yet it has great potential in the classroom. Students across content areas and grade levels are using word processing software to prepare class assignments both in the classroom and at home. Teachers are maximizing the software by using the editing functions. The editing functions allow teachers and students to monitor revisions throughout the writing process. They also are useful functions when classroom activities are based around collaborative writing assignments.

In addition to tracking revisions, word processing software has the capability to insert hypertext links, digital images, spreadsheets, and graphs. The ability to add these extensions to an assignment holds great potential for students.

Imagine how dynamic a scientific lab report can be written using these features. For instance, beyond describing the steps taken and the results found in a lab activity that documents the growth of seeds, students can insert digital images of the seeds' growth throughout the germination period. The images would be displayed in chronological order along with the student narrative that describes the activity. The students could also insert the spreadsheet that was used to document the seeds' growth. Along with the numerical data, a line graph could be inserted to help illustrate the growth. Again, student narrative would accompany the data to describe the growth. Finally, if the students have done outside research on the growth of seeds on the Internet and found resources that enrich their understanding, they could insert **hyperlinks** to the web pages with this information.

A software program that allows the user to merge audio, text, images, animation and video is multimedia software. Typically, multimedia software is interactive; that is, the user has control over the program's actions. In addition to stimulating student interest and meeting the needs of different types of learners, multimedia software allows students to create and manipulate their own multimedia presentations.

Suppose a social studies class is researching their community's local history. Students can prepare multimedia presentations that incorporate audio and video clips taken from oral history interviews of local residents, images of buildings taken years ago and today, spreadsheet data of population growth over the years, and text that depicts that summarizes the local history. The Multimedia Ethnographic Research Lab at the University of British Columbia is home to a number of multimedia projects with children. Visit their homepage to view video from sample projects and to read descriptions of their work at http://www.merlin.ubc.ca/

Presentation software allows either the teacher or students to organize information and share it with the class as a presentation. Presentation software may be linear or non-linear. Linear presentations always follow the same sequence, while non-linear presentations do not follow any particular order.

"TimeLiner" by Tom Snyder Productions is an example of linear presentation software. Teachers or students can create a timeline by entering the span of dates along with events. Textual description, images, and video clips can be added along the timeline. A science teacher might use such software to help students understand the phases of the moon. For example, students could have their own timeline of thirty days. Each day students enter text that describes the moon and inserts a digital image of the moon they took the night before. At the end of the month, students will have a recorded collection of the moon's monthly cycle.

PowerPoint is another example of linear presentation software. Teachers or students can organize text, hyperlinks, audio, images, clipart, screen shots, or video on slides to create PowerPoint presentations. PowerPoint can be an excellent tool to assist teachers with the presentation of information. The key to effectively using PowerPoint is using it to enhance classroom learning beyond the traditional slide show.

Teachers can effectively structure class discussions by putting essential or key information on a slide. This could help students monitor their own note-taking skills in that the students would not merely copy notes word-for-word off of a screen, but rather they would rather understand the major concepts and record them in their notebook. Some teachers find that printing the slide handouts is an effective way to help teach students note-taking skills.

The ability to insert objects such as audio clips and images holds great potential to enhance classroom instruction. The slides below are taken from a lesson on the Treaty of Versailles. Note that the first slide has a link to an audio file of a speech by the Secretary of War. Below the link is a series of questions to help focus the students as they listen to the audio clip. The second slide is one that the teacher presented to guide the discussion on the impact of the Treaty of Versailles.

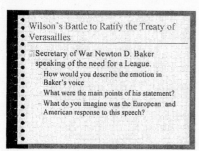 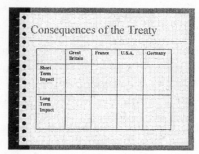

Inspiration is an example of non-linear presentation software. Inspiration is a tool that enables teachers and students to enter information and display it either as a concept map or as an outline. This is a useful piece of software to help students to map ideas and to organize their writing. Teachers may chose to prepare an Inspiration concept map to guide the class discussion or they may add to the concept map during the lesson. The example below is one that a teacher could create to guide student research on a famous person. The teacher would ask the students questions and guide their research so that they will be able to complete the concept map. After the class completes the concept map, the teacher may decide to view the information as an outline to allow the students to view the information in a linear format.

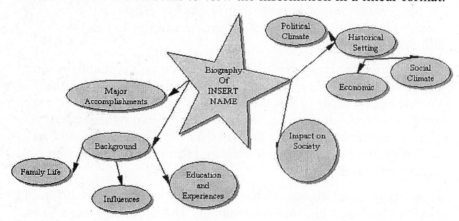

Inspiration comes with a library of clip art that may be inserted into the concept maps. There are also options that allow the user to change the display of the concept map, colors, and fonts. Kidspiration has been developed most specifically for young children. Visit http://www.inspiration.com for lesson ideas and examples.

Geometer's Sketchpad is another example of a non-linear piece of software. This software allows the user to create dynamic representations of mathematical concepts. Students are able to manipulate the representation to explore the meaning behind graphs and equations. The image below is a sample of the Pythagorean Theorem in which students manipulated the figures to arrive at an understanding of the mathematical concept. Visit http://www.keypress.com/sketchpad/ for more examples of how to use the sketchpad.

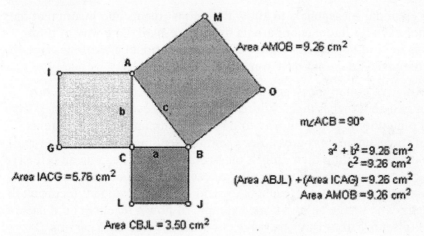

## TEACHER PRODUCTIVITY TOOLS

In addition to supporting classroom learning, technology tools can be used to enhance teacher productivity. Given the amount of time teachers dedicate to good teaching both inside and outside the classroom, productivity tools that help teachers maximize their time will also improve the quality of classroom instruction and student learning. Technology tools can help teachers communicate with parents, organize and manage information and engage in professional development opportunities.

## Communication with Parents

Teachers and parents are discovering e-mail as a new and effective method to enhance communication. Teachers and parents alike find e-mail and web pages effective means to involve parents in daily classroom activities. E-mail messages can be used to send regular information to parents about what happens in the classroom during the day. Many of today's teachers have created **listservs** and send weekly informative e-mails to their students' parents. These e-mails may contain information such as the topics covered during the week, upcoming curriculum topics, daily schedules, homework assignments and due dates, school events, as well as extended activities to be completed at home. The extended activities could include suggested readings, links to resources on the Internet, or events in the community that connect to the classroom topics (e.g. a local museum exhibit).

It is essential for teachers to know their constituents and insure that they do not exclude students or parents by using e-mail. One way of doing this is to send home print copies of all informational e-mail messages to the parents who do not have e-mail access.

Informative e-mail messages are an effective way for parents to stay informed about what their children do in school each day. Teachers also find e-mail to be a helpful way to directly communicate with parents regarding students' progress. For example, sending a brief, daily e-mail to parents regarding their child's classroom behavior can be an effective and efficient way to follow up after a teacher-parent conference. It is also an efficient way for teachers to send individual student feedback to parents. The image below is one example of how a teacher could use e-mail to send "Great Day" messages to different students' parents throughout the school year.

## A Closer Look | Using E-mail with Parents

| | |
|---|---|
| **Subject:** | Great Day! |
| **Date:** | October 21, 2002 |
| **From:** | Ms. Lane |
| **To:** | Students' Parents |

Dear Mr. and Mrs. Caldwell,

This week in class the students finished their African Art projects. Jeremy's mural is a beautiful representation of his understanding of the ancient tribes! The pictures he brought in from home look fantastic in the print. I know you will enjoy seeing his final mural. You should be very proud of Jeremy's hard work! We've placed all of the projects on display in the cafeteria. Please feel free to come and look at all of the students' art.

Sincerely,
Ms. Lane

Class web pages are another technology tool that can be used to enhance parent communication. Much like the informative e-mails, class web pages can be a place to post information that help keep parents informed about what takes place in the classroom each day and suggestions for enhancing student learning. Student work and student contributions are another feature of class web pages to include. Some teachers ask a different student each week to post a summary of the week's events on the class web page for parents to read.

## Organizational Tools

Generic software such as word processors and spreadsheets are the most commonly used organizational tools by teachers. Word processing software helps teachers generate and archive classroom materials. Lesson plans can be generated and archived according to standards taught, classroom objectives, or by unit. Teachers can revisit these lesson plans each year and easily update them and edit.

Spreadsheets or grading programs can be used to record and analyze student grades. Beyond averaging student grades at the end of the grading period, spreadsheets can help teachers analyze student grades by generating averages and distributions. Performing these calculations allows teachers to track student progress throughout the grading period.

Spreadsheets have been developed specifically to help teachers record and monitor student grades. Some schools have their own version of grade book software that allows teachers to automatically upload student grades at the end of the grading period. Other information may also be recorded in spreadsheets that can be used to help monitor student achievement, such as attendance.

Online grade books, such as GradePal (http://www.gradepal.com), have been developed for use by teachers. An added feature of using an online grade book is that parents and students may be given logins, which enable them to also monitor student progress.

A number of other software tools have been developed specifically for teachers, such as puzzle makers, rubric makers, test generators, and individualized education programs (IEPs). Again, the time a teacher saves by using one of these allows more time to be dedicated to good classroom instruction.

| *Practical Tips and Strategies* | **Teacher Tools** |
|---|---|

**Puzzlemaker** http://puzzlemaker.school.discovery.com/

**Barry's Clip Art** http://www.barrysclipart.com/

**Worksheet Generator**
http://school.discovery.com/teachingtools/worksheetgenerator/

**Flash Card Exchange** http://flashcardexchange.com/index.jsp

**Blank and Outline Maps** http://geography.about.com/cs/blankoutlinemaps/

**Certificate Creator** http://www.certificatecreator.com/

## Online Professional Development

Prior to the advent of the Internet, professional development for teachers was typically limited to local workshops that were scheduled after school hours or during the summer. The development of the Internet has ushered in numerous professional development opportunities for classroom teachers that are available any time, any place. In addition to providing teachers with professional development opportunities that are more convenient, online professional development provides teachers access to instruction not previously available and can lead to the development of online professional communities.

The number of online professional development opportunities for teachers is growing exponentially. School systems, universities, museums and other organizations are developing seminars and courses for teachers around the world. Some of these experiences are 100% online, while some use both face-to-face and online instruction. "Middle Educators Global Awareness" (MEGA) is an example of hybrid professional development. Hybrid professional development takes place both as face-to-face and online. Teachers participate in monthly workshops, but then also participate online throughout the year. For example, teachers may meet as a group to watch a demonstration on how to use GIS (geographic information systems) in the classroom. When they return to their own classrooms, they have a series of activities to complete and engage in online discussions with one another about the activities. They will meet again as a group on National GIS Day to demonstrate how they have incorporated GIS in their classroom.

Online instruction may be synchronous or asynchronous. Synchronous professional development opportunities are in real-time; for example, a videoconferencing session in which audio and video are transmitted over the Internet. The Annenberg/CPB Channel-sponsored workshop "Assessment in Math and Science: What's the Point?" is an example of synchronous professional development. In this workshop, teachers in geographically disparate locations viewed video clips about assessment strategies and then communicated directly with education experts who were in the studio for discussion about the video.

Professional development opportunities that are asynchronous are carried out over a period of time in which participants do not communicate with one another at the time. "Seminars on Science" is an example of online asynchronous professional development for teachers. This series of courses, sponsored by the National Museum of Natural Science, are taught by leading scientists to K-12 teachers across the country. The materials are web-based and provide teachers the opportunity to study with other professionals around the country and to learn about cutting-edge research. Visit "Online Professional Development: Suggestions for Success" at http://www.att.com/learningnetwork/virtualacademy/success.html to learn more about online learning and to learn more about your own learning styles.

| Practical Tips and Strategies | Sample Online Professional Development Opportunities |
|---|---|

**Concord Consortium**
http://www.concord.org

**Riverdeep Professional Development for Teachers**
http://www.riverdeep.net/pro_development/teachers_prof_dev.jhtml

**ISTE Professional Development**
http://www.iste.org/profdev/index.html

**Library of Congress Professional Development**
http://memory.loc.gov/ammem/ndlpedu/educators/index.html

**iEARN Professional Development**
http://www.iearn.org/professional/online.html

**Lesley University Online Learning**
http://www.lesley.edu/online_courses.html

# PART III: APPLICATIONS

## INQUIRY-BASED LEARNING

The previous section provided a description of a variety of technology tools. This section will look at specific applications of technology tools in the classroom. Each of the applications described is an inquiry-based lesson.

Inquiry-based learning is one of the most powerful teaching methods that technology can help facilitate. One of the essential elements of an inquiry lesson is the use of authentic data. Because the Internet provides teachers and students access to vast resources, technology promotes inquiry learning in a very powerful way. Additionally, technology tools such as spreadsheets and concept mapping software allow teachers and students to manipulate and interpret authentic data in a most effective way.

Different content areas have developed their own definitions of inquiry-based learning. However, a definition of "inquiry" developed by a team of cross-disciplinary researchers is as follows:

> Inquiry is an approach to learning that involves a process of exploring the natural or material world, that leads to asking questions and making discoveries in the search for new understandings (Exploratorium Institute for Inquiry, 1996).

Inquiry, in its purest form, requires students to play the leading role in answering questions that they themselves have asked. Molebash (2002) has outlined a "Spiral Path of Inquiry" that students should typically follow when completing an inquiry-oriented exercise.

- *Reflect* on previous or new material.
- *Ask questions* related to the topic.
- *Define procedures* for investigation.
- *Find and investigate data/information* that will help answer questions.
- *Manipulate the data/information* to answer questions.
- *Discuss* and defend results.

- *Reflect* on results...start the process over again if necessary.

As a teacher you can support student-centered inquiry. Here are some suggestions:

- Provide an interesting *hook* that students can reflect upon.

- Lead students to ask interesting *questions related to the topic.*

- When students define the procedures of their investigation, *ensure that the procedures are rigorous* enough to produce valid results.

- Assist students in *finding data resources* that will help answer their questions.

- *Provide students with access to data manipulation tools* (spreadsheet, database, or concept mapping software, etc.) as well as the prerequisite *skills* to use these tools.

Support students' efforts in presenting and defending results.

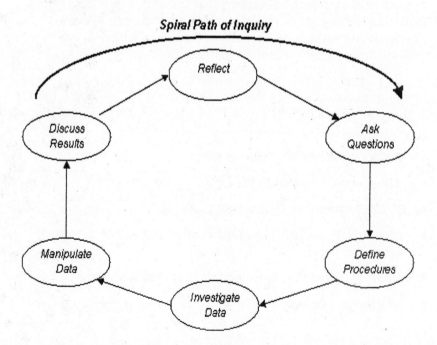

**Spiral Path of Inquiry**

# Inquiry With Numerical Data

Technology tools provide students opportunities to gather and manipulate numerical data in very effective ways. Using the Internet, probes, or other technology tools, students are able to conduct research that provides them with authentic data. Using spreadsheets, databases, or other software, students are challenged to interpret and analyze the data. Inquiry-based lessons that involve students in the manipulation of authentic data engage students in higher-order thinking activities and promote the development of critical thinking skills.

## Climate and Location

Students often do not understand the impact that latitude and longitude have on a city's climate. Using technology tools in this lesson, students will collect and analyze average temperatures from different cities and to deduce differences and similarities between their climates. This sample activity is one example of how technology tools can be used to support an inquiry-based science or math lesson.

Ask students to identify U.S. cities that are along similar lines of longitude and latitude. Sample cities are San Francisco, CA; Colorado Springs, CO; Dodge City, KS; and Norfolk, VA. Questions the teacher might ask students include: Which city is the warmest? Which city has the hottest summers? Which city is the coolest? Which city has the coolest winters? Which city gets the most snow? Which city has the lowest rainfall? While students should have conjectures for the questions posed, students may also begin to identify their own questions they would like to answer. The teacher should probe the students by asking them why they have these initial thoughts.

It is now time for students to begin researching on the Internet to start answering the questions. A suggested site to direct students to is the National Climatic Data Center (http://lwf.ncdc.noaa.gov/oa/ncdc.html). Once students locate the numerical data, they should enter it into a spreadsheet.

Working within the spreadsheet, students can calculate the mean and median monthly temperature as well as the range from the highest monthly temperature to the lowest monthly temperature. At this point the teacher should prompt the students by asking them if this is what they predicted? How do they think their calculations will appear on a line graph?

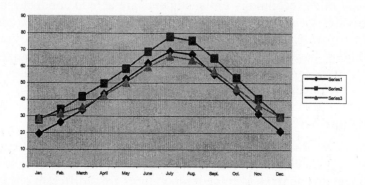

Using the graphing features of the spreadsheet software, students can create a line graph with the average monthly temperatures for each city. Once they have created the graph, ask the students to change the y-axis to highlight the extreme high and low temperatures. Students may be surprised to see how changing the y-axis can impact the data display.

From this activity, students could now conduct similar data collection and analysis of another set of cities along the same latitude or cities along similar longitudes. From their results, students should be able to hypothesize if there is a relationship between a city's location and their average temperature.

| Practical Tips and Strategies | Sample Online Sources of Numerical Data |
|---|---|

**University of Virginia's GeoStat Interactive Data**
http://fisher.lib.virginia.edu/active_data/

**Weather.com's Average Temperature and Record Temperatures**
http://www.weather.com/common/home/climatology.html

**Historical and Current Oil Market Intelligence**
http://www.energyintel.com/DataHomePage.asp?publication_id=28

**National Forest Service Inventory and Analysis**
http://www.fia.fs.fed.us/

| Practical Tips and Strategies | Sample Online Sources of Numerical Data |
|---|---|

Real Time Weather Data from the National Center for Atmospheric Research
http://www.rap.ucar.edu/weather/model/

Fleet Numerical Meteorology and Oceanography Center
http://www.fnoc.navy.mil/PUBLIC/

# Inquiry With Online Primary Sources

Using online primary sources for instruction allows students to do the same work that scholarly historians do, that is: search, discover, and analyze primary sources to learn about people, trends, and events from the past. Online primary sources may in the form of hypertext documents, video, or audio. Because of technology, students not only have access to resources outside the classroom, but they are able to interact and manipulate these sources to make meaning of them. Essentially, using digital archives in the classroom allows students to actually "do history."

In addition to accessing resources available for the classroom, students also can manipulate authentic data in a rich and meaningful way. For example, students could download documents from existing online sources, use Inspiration to create concept maps from the information they discover, or use word processing tools to write historical fiction stories or newspaper accounts. Students could even create their own online community or personal histories!

## Daily Life During the Civil War

Students are often required to memorize names, dates, and events when studying the American Civil War. Too seldom do they have the opportunity to do the work of historians and make meaning of the facts. This sample activity is one example of how technology can support an inquiry-based lesson.

The online primary sources used in this activity were digitized and archived by the University of Virginia's Virginia Center for Digital History (http://www.vcdh.virginia.edu). The Virginia Center for Digital

History is a collection of thousands of original documents related to America's history, as well as associated scholarly work placing these primary sources in an appropriate historical context.

The Valley of the Shadow Project is an online interactive archive of digitized primary sources that tells the stories of people in one southern and in one northern county before, during, and after the Civil War. Among the primary sources included in this digital history archive are letters, diaries, newspapers, census records, maps, photographs, church records, and military records. Each of these resources has either been scanned or transcribed and is accessible through the Internet.

Ask students what they know about what life was like during the Civil War, especially for someone their age. After the students generate a list of questions, direct them to the Valley of the Shadow website. Once here, students can read a series of letters written by families during this time period. These letters begin to tell the story of what life was like for everyday people during the Civil War.

The teacher should draw the students' attention to one letter, in particular. This letter is written by a young soldier to his sister at home:

From: Camp Gordonsville, Virginia

*Aug 15th, 1862*

*Dear Sister,*

*I have wanted to write home but I have not had a chance I came up to Cousin John's for some bread and while they are cooking it I thought I would write a few lines home we have been on picket ever since Tuesday and just got of this morning. . . . I am carrying the colors for the Regiment it is not as much trouble as I thought it was at first they only trouble is I have is I cannot manage my horse very well.... I have seen Ash and Mike several times but have not seen Ned but once and then I passed while he was marching and I was caring a dispatch to Gen. Jackson so I could not have much talk with him he was looking very well, how is Sister Seal I hope she is not very sick give my love to her and tell her I will write to her soon give my love to Pa, Ma, Kate and Kelly and all others who ask for me you must excuse me for not writing sooner but I have written a good many times and when I have finished I would have to go some where and would put the letter in my pocket until it was spoiled it is getting dark so I must stop I have to go 9 miles tonight so you must excuse me for not finishing this sheet.*

*Your Bro. Thos. M. Garber*

Through class discussion, the students could make a list of what they learned about Thomas Garber from reading this letter. From reading the letters, students will discover that Thomas is a soldier in the Confederate Army in the American Civil War, he needs to ride a horse to do his job, the leader of his company is C.J. O'Ferral, and he carries the flags of his regiment.

Ask students what else they would like to know about Thomas Garber and ask them for suggestions as to how they can learn more about him. Explain to students that a valuable source for learning about Americans who lived long ago is the population census. Explain to students that the census is a list made of the entire United States population every ten years. In addition to people's names, the census also records their age, occupation, place of birth, and other information. Students can use the online census tool at this website to locate census data on the Garber family.

Once students have gathered information, they could begin to interpret the primary sources and recreate the story of the Garber family. For example, after students conduct a search of the census records, they will discover Thomas was 14 in 1860, he did not own any property, he was white, and he was born in Virginia. Students could deduce that Thomas was 16 or 17 when the letters were written in 1862-1863. You might ask students if they know someone who is Thomas' age. Follow-up questions may include asking students to imagine what it would feel like to be away from home fighting in a war at this age; or asking them to hypothesize why someone of this age would be fighting in a war.

To make meaning of this historical data, students need to place the information in context and discover its relevance to their own lives. For example, students could be asked to draw a picture or write a story using the discovered information. Students are asked to write a letter from Martha Garber to Thomas Garber. In order to do this, students will need not only to show an understanding of nature of letters that were sent from the homefront to soldiers during the Civil War, but also an understanding of family life during the Civil War. By studying the Garber family letters, students will discover not only how important letters from home were and the young age of many soldiers who fought in the war, but also that one family could have three sons fighting in the Civil War.

The activity described above is one in which students are going far beyond learning about history—rather, they are *doing* history!

| Practical Tips and Strategies | Primary Sources and Hypertext Documents Online |
|---|---|

**Center for Electronic Texts in the Humanities**
http://www.ceth.rutgers.edu/

**Center for History and New Media**
http://chnm.gmu.edu/

**Documenting the American South**
http://metalab.unc.edu/docsouth/

**Electronic Text Center at the University of Virginia**
http://etext.lib.virginia.edu/

**The Geospatial and Statistical Data Center**
http://fisher.lib.virginia.edu/

**Library of Congress American Memory Project**
http://memory.loc.gov/

**Perseus Digital Library**
http://www.perseus.tufts.edu/

**Schoenberg Center for Electronic Text and Images**
http://www.library.upenn.edu/etext/

## World Languages Without Borders

Student and teacher foreign language resources have often been limited by school structures to textbooks, audiotapes, videotapes or the occasional school trip out of the country. Students who are at an entry level with their coursework often succeed in learning a world language in the classroom, but are not able to transfer the knowledge to an authentic environment. Technology tools are changing the traditional model of learning a foreign language and helping students to live within the discourse of another language.

Ask students what the current events of the day are in their community. Teachers may probe the students by asking what stories they heard on the radio or TV on the way to school or what news stories were in the morning newspaper. These could be categorized according to local, state, or national news. Questions to ask the students either through class votes or discussion include: Which news story was of most interest to you? Which story received the most press? Which stories do you want to know more about? Where could we look to learn more about these current events?

At this point, the teacher may display a web page with current news (e.g. http://www.cnn.com or http://www.nando.com). From this point, the teacher and students could learn more about the current events discussed earlier. The teacher should also ask the students to hypothesize how accessing current events from the Internet may be different that accessing them from the local radio, television, or newspaper. Students may discuss issues such as up-to-date news and different ways that the same news is portrayed.

The teacher at this juncture should guide the students towards wanting to know about current events around the world, in particular in areas where the language they are learning is spoken. Questions the teacher may ask include: What do you think are the top news stories in other areas? What differences do you think exist in how news is reported in other areas? Why do you think there might be these differences? What can we learn about other cultures by reading their news sources? How can we get access to news stories in other languages?

It is now time for students to begin researching these questions on the Internet. A suggested site to direct students to is MIT's online collection of foreign language newspapers (http://libraries.mit.edu/guides/types/flnews/). From this site, students could select one of many newspapers in a foreign language to read and interpret. Teachers may direct students to look for categories of news stories that are reported to compare the emphasis of different cultures and media sources. Teachers may also ask students to compare how world news is reported similarly or different. This could be an ongoing activity in which students record or track news stories over a period of time.

Having opportunities to practice reading a foreign language through activities such as these will help students enrich their understanding of a foreign culture and increase their vocabulary. It will also help them to understand the importance of media literacy skills and of foreign language skills in a global society.

| Practical Tips and Strategies | Sample Online World Language News Sources |
| --- | --- |

**Latin American Network Information Center**
http://lanic.utexas.edu/

**Online Newspapers**
http://www.onlinenewspapers.com/index.htm

**Voice of America (audio world news)**
http://www.voa.gov/

**CNN.com: Europe (available in different languages)**
http://europe.cnn.com/

**Editorials, Columns, and Columnists**
http://www.opinion-pages.org/

**NewsLink**
http://newslink.org/

# PART IV: EXTENSIONS

## TOMORROW'S CLASSROOMS

This guide has presented an overview of how technology tools are changing teaching and learning in today's classrooms. The technology applications explored are exemplars of how technology can be used to engage students in meaningful learning. These models should serve as springboards to guide continued exploration of the impact technology tools are having on teaching and learning.

Gordon Moore, the founder of Intel Corporation, observed that chip density doubles every eighteen months. This means that memory sizes, processor power, etc. all follow the same rate of growth. For example, today's Palm m100 has the same amount of memory as the computer that guided Apollo II to the moon in 1969. The rapid changes in technologies will continue to evolve and further change the way we teach and learn. Educators must respond to this exponential change by committing themselves to planning and implementing meaningful educational experiences for their students and engaging professional development for themselves. The resources listed below will help you continue your exploration into how technology tools can be used to enhance learning.

## BOOKS

Barre, D., Hardy, J., & Harper, D. (2001). *Generation www.Y program and curriculum guide.* Eugene, OR: International Society for Technology in Education.

Bransford, J. D., Brown, A. L., & Cocking, R. R. (Eds.) (1999). *How people learn: Brain, mind, experience, and school.* Washington, DC: National Academy Press.

Collison, G., Elbaum, B., Haavind, S., & Tinker, R. (2000). *Facilitating online learning: Effective strategies for moderators.* Madison, WI: Atwood Publishing.

Cuban, L. (2001). *Oversold and Underused: Computers in the Classroom.* Cambridge, MA: Harvard University Press.

Forcier, R.D. (2002). *The computer as an educational tool: Productivity and problem solving.* Upper Saddle River, NJ: Prentice Hall.

Grabe, M. & Grabe, C. (2001). *Integrating technology for meaningful learning.* Boston: Houghton Mifflin.

Jonassen, D. H., Peck, K.L., & Wilson, B. G. (1999). *Learning with technology: A constructivist perspective.* Columbus, OH: Prentice Hall.

Kruger, L. (2001). *Computers in the delivery of special education and related services: Developing collaborative and individualized learning environments.* New York: Haworth Press.

Moersch, C. (2002). *Beyond hardware: Using existing technology to promote higher-level thinking.* Eugene, OR: International Society for Technology in Education.

Sharp, V., Levine, M. & Sharp, R. (2002). *The best websites for teachers.* Eugene, OR: International Society for Technology in Education.

Solomon, G. & Shrum, L. (2002). *Connect online: Web learning adventures.* Columbus, OH: Glencoe/McGraw-Hill.

Williams, R. & Tollett, J. (1998). *The non-designer's web book.* Berkeley, CA: Peachpit Press.

## ARTICLES

Bull, G. L., Bull, G., Garofalo, J., & Harris, J. (2002). Grand challenges: Preparing for the technological tipping point. *Learning and Leading with Technology, 29*(8), 6–12.

Bush, G. (2001). Just sing: creativity and technology in the school library media center. *Knowledge Quest, 30* (2), 18–21.

Carroll, T. G. (2000). If we didn't have the schools we have today, would we create the schools we have today? *Contemporary Issues in Technology and Teacher Education, 1*(1). Available from http://www.citejournal.org/vol1/iss1/currentissues/general/article1.htm

Cooper, J., & Bull, G. (1997). Technology and teacher education: Past practice and recommended directions. *Action in Teacher Education, 19*(2), 97–106.

Dodge, B. (1997). Some thoughts about WebQuests. Available from http://edweb.sdsu.edu/courses/edtec596/about_webquests.html

Garofalo, J., & Pullano, F. (1997). Using graphing calculators to integrate mathematics and science. *Journal of Mathematics and Science: Collaborative Explorations, 1*(1), 53–64.

Hance, M. (2002). Playing catch-up with school technology. *Principal, (81)*5, 51–52.

Jester, R. (2002). If I had a hammer: Technology in the language arts classroom. *English Journal (91)*4, 85–88.

Means, B. (2000-2001). Technology use in tomorrow's schools. *Educational Leadership, 58*(4), 57–61.

Patterson, N. (2001). Computers and writing: feeling the power. *Voices from the Middle, 9*(1), 60–64.

Soloway, E. et al. (2001). Devices are ready-at-hand. Available from http://www.handheld.hice-dev.org/readyAtHand.htm

# WEBSITES

**International Society for Technology in Education's Teacher Resources**
http://www.iste.org/resources
*ISTE's large collection of educational resources offers listings of current Web sites, books, or periodicals that relate to educational technology.*

**Internet 101**
http://www.internet101.org/
*Created for beginners and advanced users of the Internet, this site explains the many different aspects of the Internet in a user-friendly format.*

## Bigchalk.com
http://www.bigchalk.com
*Organized into sections for teachers, parents, and students, this site is a gateway to a comprehensive collection of educational resources.*

## The George Lucas Foundation: Edutopia Online
http://www.glef.org/
*Edutopia is a collection of online videos and resources that explore effective teaching and learning in the digital age.*

## Concord Consortium
http://www.concord.org/
*This non-profit agency's web site offers a variety of educational resources, including downloads and information on handheld computing, online learning, and modeling.*

## Global Schoolhouse
http://www.gsn.org/
*The Global SchoolNet is a leader in telecollaborative projects. This site provides teachers and students opportunities to collaborate and communicate over the Internet.*

## U.S. Department of Education: Office of Education Technology
http://www.ed.gov/Technology/
*The Office of Education Technology develops and implements national educational technology policy. This site houses many different reports and resources for educators.*

## Kathy Schrock's Guide for Educators
http://school.discovery.com/schrockguide/
*One of the most extensive collections of educational resources, Kathy Schrock's Guide for Educators is a categorized list of lesson plans, professional development resources, reference materials, teacher tools, and student activities.*

# SOFTWARE

### Decisions, Decisions

*In this simulation program, students role-play a decision-maker faced with a critical situation drawn from historical events or contemporary issues. The online features allow classrooms to discuss and collaborate on the decision-making process across the Internet. Available from Tom Snyder Productions: http://www.teachtsp.com/*

### Learning to Speak Spanish

*With lessons in vocabulary, grammar, and conversation, this software teaches students Spanish from the ground up. The digital teacher feature allows students to practice their conversation by talking into a computer microphone. Available from the Learning Company: http://www.learningcompanyschool.com/*

### LEGO MINDSTORMS: Robotics Invention System 2.0

*This combination of toy LEGOs and the computer allows students to imagine and create a robot on the computer using RCX code. The infrared transmitter then lets the students test their inventions. Available from LEGO Mindstorms: http://mindstorms.lego.com/*

### Curriculum Pathways

*This product is a web-based planning environment for teachers. It allows teachers to organize and access materials quickly, plan lessons efficiently, and spend more time with students. Available from SAS in Schools: http://www.sasinschool.com/*

### Geometer's Sketch Pad

*Sketch Pad is a dynamic visualization tool that enables students to explore and understand mathematics through the process of discovery. Students can create an object and then explore its mathematical properties by clicking and dragging the mouse. Available from Key Curriculum Press: http://www.keypress.com/*

**Teacher's P.E.T.**

*This software for the handheld computer keeps track of student grades, attendance, and contact information. It is compatible with desktop spreadsheets and word processing software. Available from Palm: http://www.palm.com/*

## PROFESSIONAL ASSOCIATIONS

**The Association for Educational Communications and Technology**
1800 North Stonelake Drive, Suite 2
Bloomington, IN 47404
Phone: (812) 335-7675
Fax: (812) 335-7678
E-mail: aect@aect.org

**International Society for Technology in Education (ISTE)**
480 Charnelton Street
Eugene, OR 97401-2626
Phone: (800) 336-5191
Fax: (541) 302-3778
E-mail: iste@iste.org
Web: http://www.iste.org/

**Society for Information Technology and Teacher Education (SITE)**
P.O. Box 3728
Norfolk, VA 23514
Phone: (757) 623-7588
Fax: (703) 997-8760
E-mail: info@aace.org
Web: http://www.aace.org/site/default.htm

# FOR REFLECTION

1. How has technology changed the K–12 classroom since you were a student?

2. Visit a school and record a specific list of technology tools available and how they are used. Did the list surprise or impress you?

3. How will you continue to learn about emerging technology tools for the classroom?

4. What can you do to ensure your students are safe while using the Internet?

4. How are students different today then they were ten years ago? How can teachers respond to these differences?

6. Review the NETS for your grade level and content area. What steps can you take to meet these standards?

7. List some effective Internet search strategies.

8. How can technology tools help students learn critical thinking skills?

9. Describe what you think a school will look like ten years from now.

10. How can you use technology for professional development activities?

# GLOSSARY

**boolean search**   A method for searching that combines search terms with operators such as AND, OR, NOT. For example, "computers and art" searches for resources in which both "computers" and "art" appear.

**cyberpredators**       Individuals who seek to harm children through electronic communication.

**e-mail**  A message sent over the Internet.

**handheld**       Portable computing device that can fit in your hand.

**hyperlinks**       Text or image that will take you to information stored at another location.

**hypertext**       Documents linked in a non-linear fashion with hyperlinks.

**Internet**       A global network of computers.

**listserv** An e-mail server with a list of e-mail addresses.

**telecollaboration**       Synchronous or asynchronous communication between two or more people via the Internet.

**Web**       A part of the Internet that hosts hypertext documents.

**Web browser**  Software that enables users to access web pages.

# REFERENCES

Bergman, M. (2000). The deep web: Surfacing hidden value. Retrieved August 20, 2002 from http://www.brightplanet.com/

Exploratorium Institute for Inquiry (1996). Inquiry Descriptions. Retrieved November 5, 2002 from http://www.exploratorium.edu/IFI/resources/inquirydesc.html

Harris, J (1998). *Virtual Architecture: Designing and directing curriculum-based telecomputing.* Eugene, OR: International Society for Technology in Education.

International Society for Technology in Education (2002). *National Education Technology Standards for Teachers: Preparing teachers to use technology.* Eugene, Oregon: Author, p. 5.

Kids & media @ the new millennium: A Kaiser Family Foundation report (n.d.). Retrieved August 20, 2002, from: http://www.kff.org/content/1999/1535/pressreleasefinal.doc.html

Leiner, B., Cerf, V., Clark, D., Kahn, R., Kleinrock, L. Lynch, D., Postel, J., Roberts, L., Wolff, S. (2000). A brief history of the Internet. Retrieved September 30, 2002 from http://www.isoc.org/internet/history/brief.shtml

Levin, D. & Arefeh, S. (2002). *The digital disconnect: The widening gap between Internet-savvy students and their schools.* Pew Internet & American Life. Retrieved August 30, 2002 from http://www.pewinternet.org/reports/pdfs/PIP_Schools_Internet_Rep ort.pdf

Molebash, P., & Dodge, B. (2002). *WebQuests vs. inquiry: Whose question is it, anyway?* Paper presented at the Computer-Using Educators State Conference, Anaheim, CA.

Skinner, R. (2002). Tracking Tech Trends. *Technology Counts 2002: E-Defining Education, 21*(35), 53–56. Retrieved August 20, 2002 from http://www.edweek.org/sreports/tc02/article.cfm?slug=35tracking.h 21